PIANO / VOCAL / GUITAR

budgetbooks

LATIN SONGS

Exclusive Distributors:
Music Sales Limited
14-15 Berners Street, London W1T 3LJ

Order No. HLE90002484
ISBN 1-84609-124-1
This book © Copyright 2005 by Hal Leonard Europe

Printed in the EU

Your Guarantee of Quality
As publishers, we strive to produce every book to the highest commercial standards.
The book has been carefully designed to minimise awkward page turns and to make playing from it a real pleasure.
Throughout, the printing and binding have been planned to ensure a sturdy, attractive publication which should give years of enjoyment.
If your copy fails to meet our high standards, please inform us and we will gladly replace it.

www.musicsales.com

HLE
Hal Leonard Europe
Distributed by Music Sales

CONTENTS

A FELICIDADE

Words and Music by VINICIUS DE MORAES,
ANDRE SALVET and ANTONIO CARLOS JOBIM

ACÉRCATE MÁS
(Come Closer To Me)

Original Words and Music by OSVALDO FARRES
English Words by AL STEWART

ADIÓS

English Words by EDDIE WOODS
Spanish Translation and Music by ENRIC MADRIGUERA

We were so hap-py, dear, to-geth-er, ___ and ev-'ry dream of joy ___ we knew. ___
Ya la a-le - grí-a de ___ mi vi-da ___ es co-mo un sue-ño que ___ se va ___

___ A cas-tle in the air, ___ dear, for - ev-er, ___ a world of love for just ___ we two. ___
por-que al lle-gar de nue - vo el dí-a ___ con mi i-lu - sión me he de a - le-jar ___

12

AHORA SEREMOS FELICES
(La Casita)

Words and Music by
RAFAEL HERNÁNDEZ

Yo ten-go ya la ca-si-ta   que tan-to te pro-me-
Pa-ra com-ple-tar la di-cha   y nues-tra fe-li-ci-

tí, _____   y lle-na de mar-ga-ri-tas   pa-ra tí, _____
dad, _____   ha-ce fal-ta u-na co-si-ta   que se-rá _____

AQUELLOS OJOS VERDES
(Green Eyes)

Music by NILO MENENDEZ
Spanish Words by ADOLFO UTRERA
English Words by E. RIVERA and E. WOODS

Life held no charm, dear, un-til I met you.
Fue - ron tus o - jos los que me die - rón

ALWAYS IN MY HEART
(Siempre En Mi Corazón)

Music and Spanish Words by ERNESTO LECUONA
English Words by KIM GANNON

AMOR
(Amor, Amor, Amor)

Music by GABRIEL RUIZ
Spanish Words by RICARDO LÓPEZ MÉNDEZ
English Words by NORMAN NEWELL

Tempo di Beguine

A - mor,   a - mor,   a -
A - mor,   *a - mor,*   *a -*

mor. _____   That's how I say   the lat - in way   how much I
mor. _____   *Na - ció de tí,*   *na - ció de mí,*   *de la es pe -*

love you. _____   A - mor,   a - mor,   a -
ran - za. _____   *A - mor,*   *a - mor,*   *a -*

29

AND I LOVE HER

Words and Music by JOHN LENNON
and PAUL McCARTNEY

AUNQUE ME CUESTE LA VIDA

Words and Music by
LUIS KALAFF

8va Lower.

BAIA
(Bahía)

Music and Portuguese Lyric by ARY BARROSO
English Lyric by RAY GILBERT

40

42

BÉSAME MUCHO
(Kiss Me Much)

Music and Spanish Words by
CONSUELO VELAZQUEZ
English Words by SUNNY SKYLAR

BOSSA NOVA BABY

Words and Music by JERRY LEIBER
and MIKE STOLLER

48

BRAZIL

Original Words and Music by ARY BARROSO
English Lyrics by S.K. RUSSELL

CALL ME

Words and Music by
TONY HATCH

If you're feel-ing sad and lone-ly, there's a serv-ice I can ren-der. Tell the one who loves you on-ly, I can be so warm and ten-der. Call me!

COPACABANA
(At The Copa)

Music by BARRY MANILOW
Lyric by BRUCE SUSSMAN and JACK FELDMAN

Moderately, with a Latin feel

62

CAMINO DE GUANAJUATO

Words and Music by
JOSÉ ALFREDO JIMÉNEZ

Additional Lyrics

3. Camino de Guanajuato
   Que pasas por tanto pueblo
   No pasas por Salamanca
   Que allí me dieren recuerdo
   Me te rodean de vereas
   No pasa porque me vuelo.

4. El Cristo de la montana
   Cel cerro del Cubilete
   Consuelo do los que sufren
   Adoracion de las gentes
   El Cristo de la montana
   Del cerro del Cubilete.

5. Camino de Santa Rosa
   La sierra de Guanajuato
   Alli nomas tras lomita
   Se ve Dolores Hidalgo
   Yo alli me quedo paisano
   Alli es mi pueblo adorado.

CHEGA DE SAUDADE
(No More Blues)

English Lyric by JON HENDRICKS and JESSIE CAVANAUGH
Original Text by VINICIUS DE MORAES
Music by ANTONIO CARLOS JOBIM

74

THE CONSTANT RAIN
(Chove Chuva)

Original Words and Music by JORGE BEN
English Words by NORMAN GIMBEL

CORAZÓN CORAZÓN

Words and Music by
JOSE MA. NAPOLEON

Con-tra vien-to y __ ma-re-a lu-cha-ré. __ Por te-

ner tus lin-dos o-jos ven-ce-ré. Por tu a-

mor no ha-brá __ dis-tan-cia, si es por tí ca-mi-na-ré. __ Vol-re-

Additional Lyrics

2. Donde vayas he de ir contigo, amor.
Si una mano necesitas dos tendré,
Y si sufres una pena,
Una pena sufriré.
Cuando rías a tu lado reiré.
To Chorus

3. Cuando nos quedemos solos otra vez,
Porque tengan nuestros hijios que crecer.
Tal vez yo te invite al cine.
Y en lo oscuro como ayer,
Algun beso en la mejilla te daré.
To Chorus

CUANTO LE GUSTA

Original Words and Music by GABRIEL RUIZ
English Words by RAY GILBERT

86

87

A DAY IN THE LIFE OF A FOOL
(Manhã De Carnaval)

Words by CARL SIGMAN
Music by LUIZ BONFA

91

92

DESAFINADO
(Off Key)

English Lyric by GENE LEES
Original Text by NEWTON MENDONÇA
Music by ANTONIO CARLOS JOBIM

99

DON'T CRY FOR ME ARGENTINA

from EVITA

Words by TIM RICE
Music by ANDREW LLOYD WEBBER

101

look at me to know that ev - 'ry word is true. ___

poco rit.

EL CUMBANCHERO

Words and Music by
RAFAEL HERNÁNDEZ

cum - ba, cum - ba, cum - ba, cum - ban - che - ro.

A bon - go, bon - go, bon - go, bon - go - se - ro.

109

EL TRISTE

Words and Music by
ROBERTO CANTORAL

THE END OF A LOVE AFFAIR

Words and Music by
EDWARD C. REDDING

THE FOOL ON THE HILL

Words and Music by JOHN LENNON
and PAUL McCARTNEY

Day af-ter day, a-lone on a hill, ___ The
Well on the way, head in a cloud, ___ The

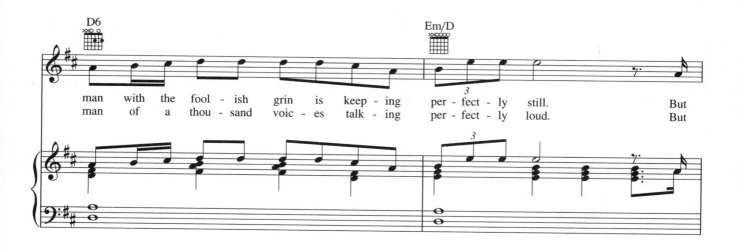

man with the fool-ish grin is keep-ing per-fect-ly still. But
man of a thou-sand voic-es talk-ing per-fect-ly loud. But

no-bod-y wants to know ___ him, They can see that he's just ___ a fool. ___ And
no-bod-y ev-er hears ___ him, Or the sound he ap-pears ___ to make. ___ And

FRENESÍ

Words and Music by
ALBERTO DOMINGUEZ

GRANADA

Spanish Words and Music by AGUSTÍN LARA
English Words by DOROTHY DODD

THE GIFT!
(Recado Bossa Nova)

Music by DJALMA FERREIRA
Original Lyric by LUIZ ANTONIO
English Lyric by PAUL FRANCIS WEBSTER

THE GIRL FROM IPANEMA
(Garôta De Ipanema)

Music by ANTONIO CARLOS JOBIM
English Words by NORMAN GIMBEL
Original Words by VINICIUS DE MORAES

144

HOW INSENSITIVE
(Insensatez)

Music by ANTONIO CARLOS JOBIM
Original Words by VINICIUS DE MORAES
English Words by NORMAN GIMBEL

How ___ un-moved ___ and cold ___
Vague ___ and drawn ___ and sad, ___

___ I must ___ have seemed ___ when { he / she } told me so ___ sin - cere-
___ I see ___ it still, ___ all { his / her } heart-break in ___ that last ___

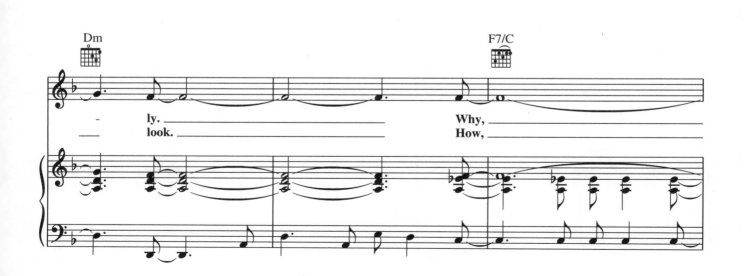

- ly. ___ Why, ___
___ look. ___ How, ___

148

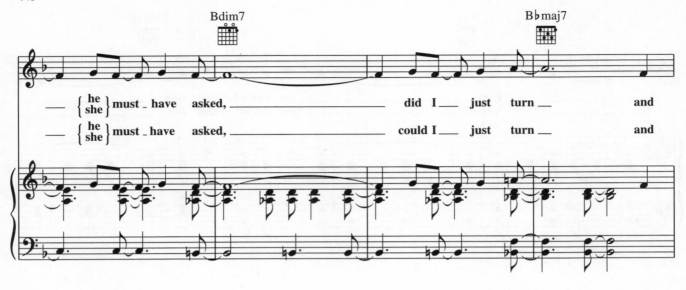

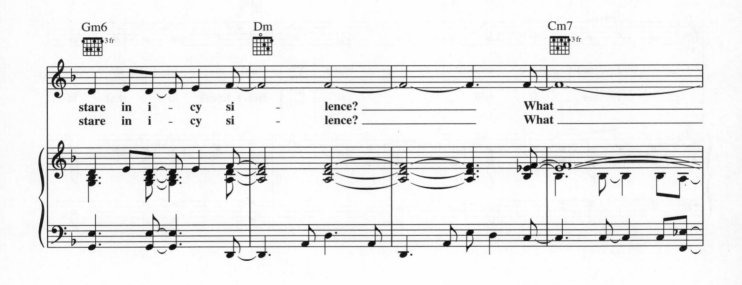

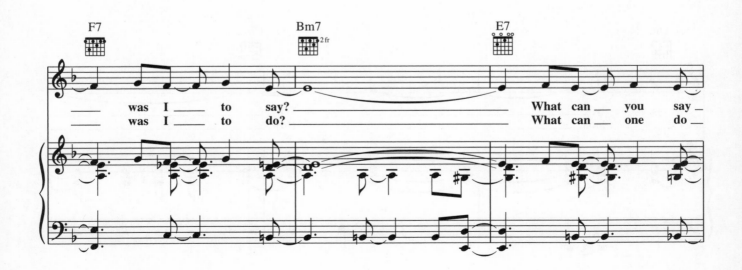

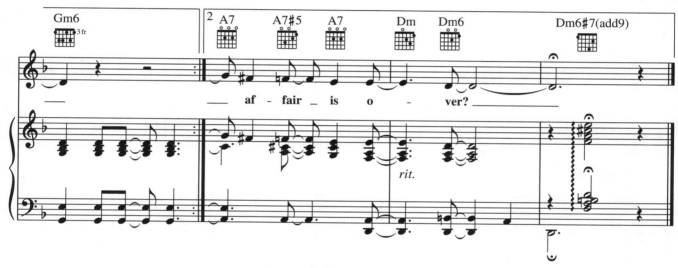

Portuguese Lyrics

A insensatez
Que você fez
Coração mais sem cuidado
Fez chorar de dôr
O seu amôr
Um amôr tão delicado
Ah! Porque você
Foi fraco assim
Assim tão desalmado
Ah! Meu coração
Que nunca amou
Não merece ser amado
Vai meu coração
Ouve a razão
Usa só sinceridade
Quem semeia vento
Diz a razão
Colhe tempestade
Vai meu coração
Pede perdão
Perdão apaixonado
Vai porque
Quem não
Pede perdão
Não é nunca perdoado.

INOLVIDABLE

Words and Music by
JULIO GUTIERREZ

KISS OF FIRE

Words and Music by LESTER ALLEN
and ROBERT HILL
Adapted from A.G. VILLOLDO

LA BAMBA

By RITCHIE VALENS

Moderate Latin Rock beat

LA BARCA

Words and Music by
ROBERTO CANTORAL

Di - cen que __ la dis - tan - cia es el ol - vi - do, ____

____ pe - ro yo __ no con - ci - bo e - sa ra - zón.

Por - que yo __ se - gui - ré sien - do el cau -

mi los su - fri - mien - tos _____ en la pri - me - ra

no - che que te a - mé. _____

Hoy mi pla - ya se vis - te de a - mar - gu - ra _____
Cuan - do la ___ luz del sol se es - te a - pa - gan - do _____

por que tu ___ bar - ca tie - ne que par -
y te sien - tas can - sa - da de va -

LA FLOR DE LA CANELA

Words and Music by
ISABEL GRANADA Y LARCO

166

rí - o y al vien-to la lan-za-ba del puen — te a la A - la - me - da.___

Dé-ja-me que te cuen-te, li - me - ño Ay! De-ja que te di-ga mo-re-no___

___ mi pen - sa - mien - to, ___ a ver si a-sí des - pier-tas del

sue - ño del sue-ño que en-tre-tie-ne, mo-re - no, tu sen-ti - mien - to.___

168

LA ÚLTIMA NOCHE

Words and Music by
ROBERTO (BOBBY) COLLAZO

LA MALAGUEÑA

By ELPIDIO RAMIREZ
and PEDRO GALINDO

¡Qué bo - ni - tos o - jos tie - nes___ de - ba - jo de e - sas dos ce - jas,___ de
Si por po - bre me des - pre - cias,___ yo te con - ce - do ra - zón,___ yo

LA PALOMA

English Lyrics by MARJORIE HARPER
Music and Spanish Lyrics by D. DE YRADIER
Arranged by R. ROSAMOND JOHNSON

177

178

2.

I'll give you my hand, with all of the love I own;

I'll live all my life for you and you alone;

We'll go to church for blessings that wait in store,

And so - there'll be one where two had been before.

3.

The day we are married, we'll tell the world "Goodbye,"

Away we will go together, you and I.

But when time has passed us by with each coming year,

'Tis then, many little Gauchos will appear.

2.

El dia que nos casemos
Valgame Dios!
En la semana que hay ir
Me hace reir
Desde la Yglesia juntitos
Que si senor
Nos hiremos a dormir
Alla voy yo
Si a tu ventana llega etc.

3.

Cuando el curita nos seche
La bendicion
En la Yglesia Catrédal
Alla voy yo
Yo te duré la manita
Con mucho amor
Y el cura dos hisopazos
Que si senor
Si a tu ventana llega etc.

LITTLE BOAT

Original Words by RONALDO BOSCOLI
English Words by BUDDY KAYE
Music by ROBERTO MENESCAL

183

LOVE ME WITH ALL YOUR HEART
(Cuando Calienta El Sol)

Original Words and Music by CARLOS RIGUAL
and CARLOS A. MARTINOLI
English Words by SUNNY SKYLAR

186

MAÑANA

Words and Music by PEGGY LEE
and DAVE BARBOUR

See additional lyrics

188

ña - na, _____ ma - ña - na, _____

ma - ña - na ___ is soon e - nough ___ for

me.   My

Additional Lyrics

3. Oh, once I had some money but I gave it to my friend.
   He said he'd pay me double, it was only for a lend.
   But he said a little later that the horse she was so slow.
   Why he gave the horse my money is something I don't know.

4. My brother took his suitcase and he went away to school.
   My father said he only learn'd to be a silly fool.
   My father said that I should learn to make a chili pot.
   But then I burn'd the house down the chili was too hot.

5. The window she is broken and the rain is coming in.
   If someone doesn't fix it I'll be soaking to my skin.
   But if we wait a day or two the rain may go away.
   And we don't need a window on such a sunny day.

MAMBO JAMBO
(Que Rico El Mambo)

English Words by RAYMOND KARL and CHARLIE TOWNE
Original Words and Music by DÁMASO PÉREZ PRADO

194

MAMBO #5

Words and Music by
DAMASO PEREZ PRADO

Sí,   sí,   sí,   yo quie - ro   mam - bo!

A MAN AND A WOMAN
(Un Homme Et Une Femme)
from A MAN AND A WOMAN

Original Words by PIERRE BAROUH
English Words by JERRY KELLER
Music by FRANCIS LAI

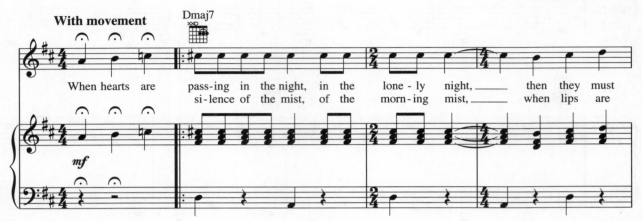

When hearts are pass-ing in the night, in the lone-ly night, _____ then they must
si-lence of the mist, of the morn-ing mist, _____ when lips are

hold each oth-er tight, Oh, so ver-y tight _____ and take a chance that in the light, in to-
wait-ing to be kissed, long-ing to be kissed, _____ where is the rea-son to re-sist and de-

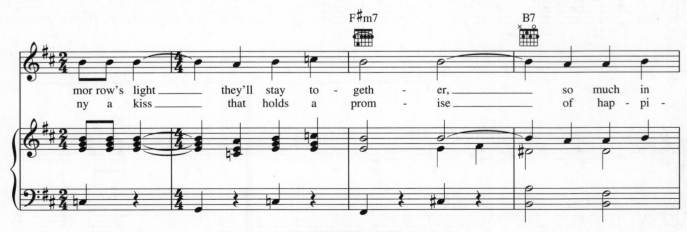

mor row's light _____ they'll stay to-geth-er, _____ so much in
ny a kiss _____ that holds a prom-ise _____ of hap-pi-

MARÍA ELENA

English Words by S.K. RUSSELL
Music and Spanish Words by LORENZO BARCELATA

Like fall - ing rain to a flow'r, ____
Quie - ro can - tar - te, mu - jer,

Or like the shore to the sea; ____
mi más bo - ni - ta can - ción.

Like min - utes are to an hour, ____
Por - que e - res tú mi que - rer,

207

MAS QUE NADA

Words and Music by
JORGE BEN

MEDITATION
(Meditacão)

Music by ANTONIO CARLOS JOBIM
Original Words by NEWTON MENDONÇA
English Words by NORMAN GIMBEL

NOCHE DE RONDA
(Be Mine Tonight)

Original Words and Music by MARÍA TERESA LARA
English Words by SUNNY SKYLAR

* English: skip to **

216

218

MUJER

Words and Music by
AGUSTÍN LARA

Mu- jer, _____ mu- jer di- vi- na, _____ tie-nes el ve- ne- no que fas- ci- na en tu mi-

221

OBSESIÓN

Words and Music by
PEDRO FLORES

ONCE I LOVED
(Amor Em paz)
(Love In Peace)

Music by ANTONIO CARLOS JOBIM
Portuguese Lyrics by VINICIUS DE MORAES
English Lyrics by RAY GILBERT

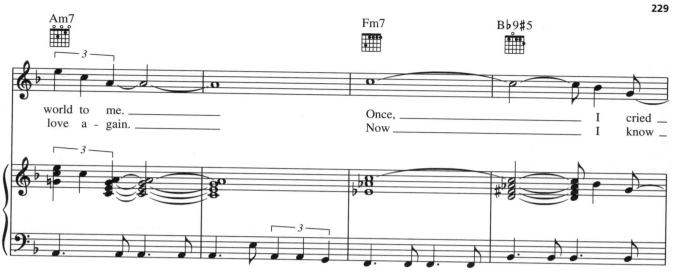

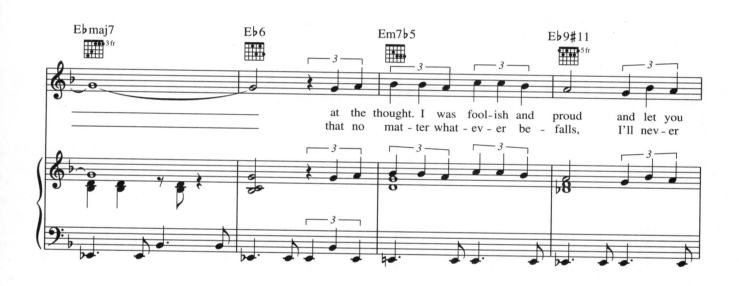

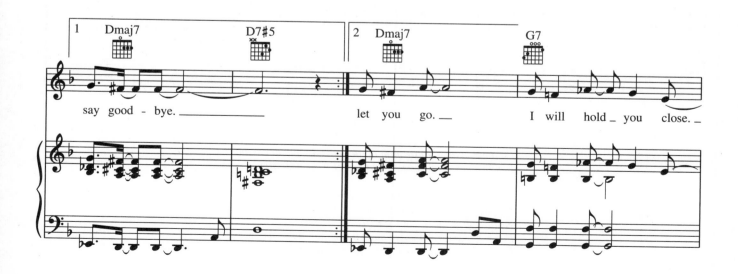

230

Portuguese Lyrics

Eu amei, e amei ai de mim muito mais do que devia amar.
E chorei ao sentir que eu iria sofrer e me desesperar.

Foi então, que da minha infinita triztesa aconteceu você.
Encontrei, em você a razão de viver e de amar em paz
E não sofrer mais. Nunca mais.
Porque o amor é a coisa mais triste quando se desfaz.
O amor é a coisa mais triste quando se desfaz.

ONE NOTE SAMBA
(Samba De Uma Nota So)

Original Lyrics by NEWTON MENDONCA
English Lyrics by ANTONIO CARLOS JOBIM
Music by ANTONIO CARLOS JOBIM

This is just a lit - tle sam - ba built up - on a sin - gle note.

Oth - er notes are bound to fol - low, but the root is still that note.

Now the new one is the con - se - quence of the one we've just been through,

ONLY TRUST YOUR HEART

Words by SAMMY CAHN
Music by BENNY CARTER

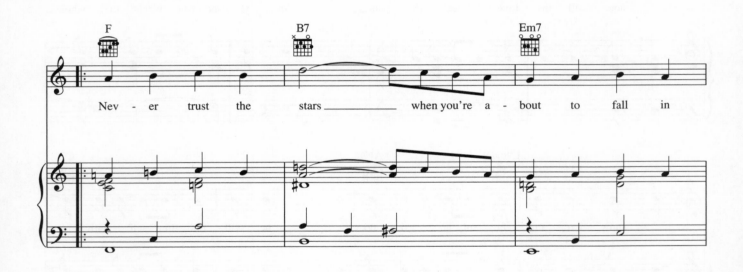

Nev - er trust the stars _____ when you're a - bout to fall in love.

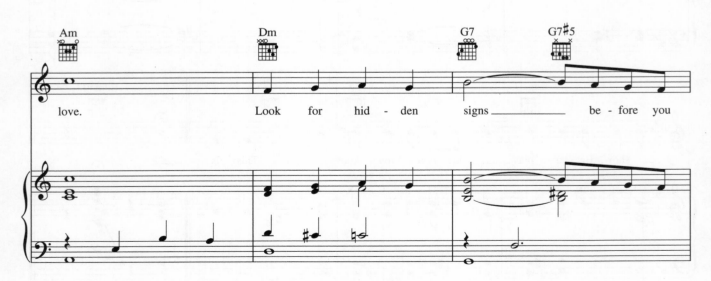

love. Look for hid - den signs _____ be - fore you

PATRICIA, IT'S PATRICIA
(Patricia)

English Words by BOB MARCUS
Original Music by DÁMASO PÉREZ PRADO

240

PERDÓN

Words and Music by
PEDRO FLORES

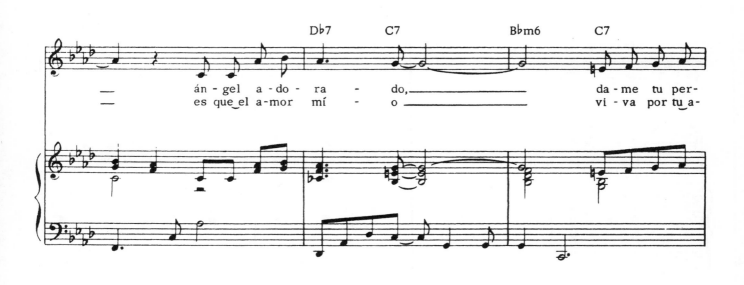

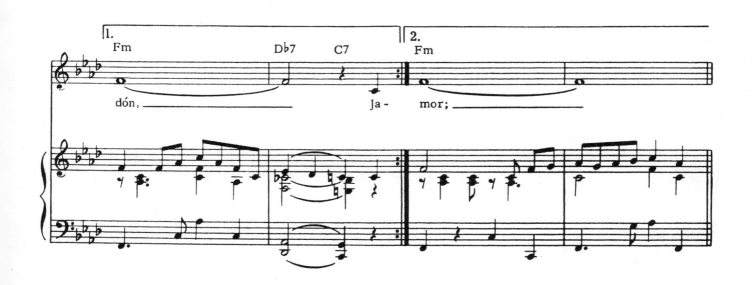

246

PERFIDIA

Words and Music by
ALBERTO DOMINGUEZ

QUIZÁS, QUIZÁS, QUIZÁS
(Perhaps, Perhaps, Perhaps)

Original Words and Music by
OSVALDO FARRES
English Words by JOE DAVIS

QUIET NIGHTS OF QUIET STARS
(Corcovado)

English Words by GENE LEES
Original Words & Music by ANTONIO CARLOS JOBIM

SABOR A MÍ
(Be True To Me)

Original Words and Music by ALVARO CARRILLO
English Words by MEL MITCHELL

SAMBA DE ORFEU

Words by ANTONIO MARIA
Music by LUIZ BONFA

SABRÁS QUE TE QUIERO

Words and Music by
TEDDY FREGOSO

Cuan - do pue - dan mis no - ches ha - blar - te y lo - gren de -

cír - te lo que e - res en mí, qué de co - sas i - rán a con -

tar - te, cuan - tas o - tras sa - brás tú de mí. Que te

SÓ DANÇO SAMBA

(Jazz 'N' Samba)

from the film COPACABANA PALACE

English Lyric by NORMAN GIMBEL
Original Text by VINICIUS DE MORAES
Music by ANTONIO CARLOS JOBIM

The jazz 'n' sam-ba, the jazz 'n' sam-ba,
Só dan-ço sam-ba, só dan-ço sam-ba.

hear it all a-round, ___ the jazz 'n' sam-ba, the jazz 'n'
Vai, vai, vai, vai, vai! ___ Só dan-ço sam-ba, só dan-ço

sam-ba sound. ___ The
sam-ba. Vai! ___ Só

271

SO NICE
(Summer Samba)

Original Words and Music by MARCOS VALLE
and PAULO SERGIO VALLE
English Words by NORMAN GIMBEL

Some-one to hold me tight, that would be ver - y nice, some-one to love me right, that would be ver - y nice. Some-one to un-der-stand each lit-tle dream__ in me, some-one to take my hand, to be a team__ with me. So nice,_____

SONG OF THE JET
(Samba Do Avião)

English Lyric by GENE LEES
Original Text and Music by ANTONIO CARLOS JOBIM

278

Portuguese Lyrics

Minha alma canta. Vejo o Rio de Janeiro.
Estou morrendo de saudade.
Rio, teu mar, praias sem fim,
Rio, você foi feito pra mim.
Cristo Redentor, braços abertos sobre a Guanabara.
Este samba é só porque,
Rio, eu gosto de você.
A morena vai sambar,
Seu corpo todo balançar.
Rio de sol, de céu, de mar,
Dentro de mais um minuto estaremos no Galeão.
Cristo Redentor, braços abertos sobre a Guanabara.
Este samba é só porque,
Rio, eu gosto de você.
A morena vai sambar,
Seu corpo todo balançar.
Aperte o cinto, vamos chegar.
Agua brilhando, olha a pista chegando,
E vamos nós,
Aterrar.

SWAY
(Quien Será)

English Words by NORMAN GIMBEL
Spanish Words and Music by PABLO BELTRAN RUIZ

When ma-rim-ba rhy-thms start to play, dance with me,
Quien se-rá la que me quie-ra a mí Quien se-rá

make me sway. _ Like the la-zy o-cean hugs the shore,
Quien se-rá____ Quien se-rá la que me dé su a-mor

hold me close, sway me more. _____ Like a flow-er bend-ing
Quien se-rá Quien se-rá_____ Yo no sé si la po-

TRES PALABRAS
(Without You)

Original Words and Music by OSVALDO FARRES
English Words by RAY GILBERT

Lyrics:

I'm so lone-ly and blue, _____ when I'm with-
out you. _____ I don't know what I'd do, _____
sweet-heart, with-out you. _____ The joy and

O- ye la con-fe - sión, _____ de mi se-
cre - to, _____ na - ce de un co-ra - zón
que es - tá de - sier - to; Con tres pa -

TABOO

Words and Music by
MARGARITA LECUONA

TANGO OF ROSES

Words by MARJORIE HARPER
Music by VITTORIO MASCHERONI

THIS MASQUERADE

Words and Music by
LEON RUSSELL

*Guitar solo sounds 8va
lower than written.

quer - ade._____

TICO TICO
(Tico Tico No Fuba)

Words and Music by ZEQUINHA ABREU,
ALOYSIO OLIVEIRA and ERVIN DRAKE

300

TIME WAS

English Words by S.K. RUSSELL
Music by MIGUEL PRADO

303

TRISTE

By ANTONIO CARLOS JOBIM

Sad __ is to live in sol - i - tude __

far __ from your tran - quil al - ti - tude. __

Portuguese Lyrics:

Triste é viver a na solidão
Na dor cruel de uma paixão
Triste é saber que ninguem pade viver de ilusão
Que nunca vai ser, nunca dar
O sonhador tem que acordar.

Tua beleza é um auião
Demals pra um pobre coracao
Que para pra te ver passar
So pra se maltratar
Triste é viver na solidãd.

TÚ SÓLO TÚ

By FELIPE VALDES LEAL

VAYA CON DIOS
(May God Be With You)

Words and Music by LARRY RUSSEL,
INEZ JAMES and BUDDY PEPPER

Moderate Waltz Tempo

WATCH WHAT HAPPENS
from THE UMBRELLAS OF CHERBOURG

Music by MICHEL LEGRAND
Original French Text by JACQUES DEMY
English Lyrics by NORMAN GIMBEL

YELLOW DAYS

English Lyric by ALAN BERNSTEIN
Music and Spanish Lyric by ALVARO CARRILLO

WAVE

Words and Music by
ANTONIO CARLOS JOBIM

Portuguese Lyrics

Vou te contar, os olhos já não podem ver,
Coisas que só o coração pode entender.
Fundamental é mesmo o amor,
É impossível ser feliz sozinho.

O resto é mar, é tudo que não sei contar.
São coisas lindas, que eu tenho pra te dar.
Vem de mansinho abrisa e mediz,
É impossível ser feliz sozinho.

Da primeira vez era a cidade,
Da segunda o cais e a eternidade.

Agora eu já sei, da onda que se ergueu no mar,
E das estrelas que esquecemos de contar.
O amor se deixa surpreender,
Enquanto a noite vem nos envolver.

YOU BELONG TO MY HEART
(Solamente Una Vez)

Original Words and Music by AGUSTIN LARA
English Words by RAY GILBERT

Moderately

You be-long to my heart ____
So-la-men-te u-na vez ____

____ now and for-ev-er, ____ and our love had its
____ a-mé en la vi-da, ____ so la-men-te u-na

start ____ not long a-go.
vez ____ y na-da más. ____

YOURS
(Cuando Se Quiere De Veras)

Words by ALBERT GAMSE and JACK SHERR
Music by GONZALO ROIG

Yours till the stars lose their glo-ry,

yours till the birds fail to sing.